Mont-Saint-Jean

D1679699

Other Books by Lyndon Davies:

Hyphasis
Shield
A Colomber in the House of Poesy
Bridge 116
Canalchemy: The Materials
Reset (*selected earlier poems*)
The Man Who Painted Mountains (Play)
Resemblance (Selected Prose)

Mont-Saint-Jean

For Gavin,

With very best wishes

Lyn
x

Lyndon Davies

AQUIFER

Published in the United Kingdom in 2022 by

Aquifer Books,
www.glasfrynproject.org.uk

ISBN: 978-1-8383587-7-8

Cover image: Penny Hallas (from *Poète Assassiné* series)
Cover Design: Aquifer

Contents

For John Goodby

Mont-Saint-Jean

"Quelle affaire!" (Marshall Blücher)

"They have altered my field of battle!" (The Duke of
Wellington in Victor Hugo's *Les Misérables*)

Prologue

A Ball

1

There must be a prologue
we join hands we circle
around and then back again

many jostling and skittish
but as for the prologue maker
still just a pivot short

of a skip, it's the weight
of that first modern chord hammered
drawing all to attention here

2

Belief in the candour
of what we call address
rigadoon to the right

and to the left ditto
each unimagined universe
never the same quark once

though founded on repetition
the steps known
by resolution without reflection

3

Half around then reverse
and back to the starting gate
after that it's a question

when the forms firm
what the feelers tell us
waiting in anticipation

right hand and now left
across it, pre-configuring
twitch of a later turn

4

Perhaps a star is born
measured out symmetrically
by four by eight

first balance at the centre
chain around by right
then promenade clapping

turning to face each other
changes upon fancy
for pleasure to curtail it

5

Some plunging deep into muddle
at the end of a room
just beyond the candle-sweat

fatigue getting the better of them
in general, that slow fade
of a clown's genome

then coming back ravaged into figure
from depravity of shadows
wit rising in defiance

6

In the fingers that reach for us
a stiffening impress of laws
applied macrocosmically

as if an entire history
begins with a frisson
sparked from two celibate engines

of overheated gristle chafed
through a common knot, well anyway
it's a stepping off point

7

The geography is well known
reconnoitered thoroughly
set down as a diagram

arrows in space, even if only
sketched on a piece of paper
real shapes that a world holds

internally as if brought up to it
useful in a functional way
not necessarily coercive

8

Do we know if it's sufficient though
simply to carry through
on a full set of variations

capering on clunched
to the bounds, such passion pledged
to inaugurate a hedge

scattered flowers on each jalon
tracery of imprints in the hallowed turf
tasers at two metres

9

We have gone around and come back
and linked arms and steepled
whatever it took

yes the future is waiting
but only in note form
fallible and the past

this knee on the neck
is there anywhere to speak anywhere
what oxygen in the interim

10

What began as a prologue
now terminates in a state
of premonitory destitution

though itself already branching
beyond specification
beyond advice list or liturgy

couples spruce as new cotton buds
bounce through a wizening landscape
delirium in each quip and jink of it

L'Affaire

The Thing in Itself

11

The sad rain the *olden*
falling on so much night
so much unreadiness

no rest for the wicked now
or those to be wicked later
in the early time

the olden the early
sick earth clinching us slack
into hungers our own dark

12

Shaking the maps out
better to watch than sleep
to assert one's enemy

in the wakeful where
of it, anyone engaged snug
averse to reveal unearthed

there as offering of sufficient
fit, spread aura smudging pale
sparks over intermittent ridge

13

No requirement for knowledge here
nor gloss where the dawn curbs
all reason with what it costs

no requirement for comprehension
as integration where the mud
envelops us, fair play

all settled and accepted
lifting our riddled heads
to the sun man-marigolds

14

Tracts synchronous recline
under light now any brow
better than no brow

death couldn't find us
lay snuggling into luck
then death found us

stand up anyway
when the high come shrieking
definitive messengers

15

Quite ready then but crust unstable
wheels retch in the slubbered
folklore of a general plan

blots everywhere, any arrow
immediately sucked off by its own target
keep trampling the ditch

foundation gradually packs solid
enough to permit
action by disembodied wisps

16

All 'subsidiary' lobes momentarily
deflated or strapped tight
to a fixed armature

driving the work through
just one lobe to be monster
with and no other

impossible to recognise what was lost
until later no longer
credible or like a tale of sorts

17

Nothing but your scrawled name that
on a paper duly
to be pulped anyway

by rain by blood flummoxed
metal spatchcocked or by fire
duly (tr)ashed

her name his name
on a scrap or a passing smoke-twirl
holy no reply needed

18

Pressure beating up the slope
bunched vessel of high tone
head on insoluble

some clipped fringe spitting back
at it where it is not looked
for great upset

adjustments querulous
calculations entering
as skewed equation

19

Protect as abstraction
one symbol above anything
withhold under stress

devotion of special converts
wrought up or momentarily
plucked from a ring of wavers

threat nags, semiotic
drags as it's grappled back
under wraps, torn as hope

20

In the middle a true chore
either wall of a clear corridor
imagined ahead of loss

keeps aching and will not let peace come
river poured down
a pulse like a beaten drum

so steady unperturbed
by incursions, this
merely following that

21

Supply where necessary
somehow it doesn't matter
what's broken in this service

the numerology of a risk
debated under cover
of smashed hedgerow, a deep way

with indifferent insects
resolving into the open
your inexorable commission

22

Coming from all directions
bounce if they do some
or not before taken

bounce there's another
don't flex even vestigially
not done for good reason

looks spent anyway
don't try sir and put
your foot on it

23

Just a bit speeded up is all
but still shocking that beam shot
through blood's dreaming wall

by quick turns lit then severally
reconfigured, each clean swath
just a bit speeded up

slot opens raying through
into lesion, is seen lack
then a vent shuts

24

That's to say what we stand up for
would bow if they let us
by even as little as an inch

low polities stacked incremental
malice humped junk
got up in its motley

machinery of the unassuagable
pointed at you at me
from either side of an erasion zone

25

Plumed flailing up over the ridge
more lustered than what's struck
and freer to throw gestures

biting at first
more dreaded than efficacious
then eventually quite relaxing

which comes and spends itself
in surge after surge, a spooked lull
pierced only by common voices

26

Some primal pattern
of correspondences, even if not complete
or clear through the moving pillars

drifts through the precinct met
by a solemn functionary bearing the latest
mock-up from the outer limits

does anything here match
can we make it match if we take it away and work on it
botch and return to printer

27

This then reimagined as proleptic widget
and distributed in the field
like a Yule parcel coming all at once, hey a parcel

bearing its sigil of authority
you cuddle it on your stomach
warm and settling like a dream of plenty

though never to unwrap as parcel
as if to preserve the mystery
could redeem the hour

28

Music sweet mummery
of crimped will schmoozing over
wooing us to an elevated lurch

a pulse and the lobe throbs
at once into position as
sole arbiter in a floating annex

by rhythm generated, viced
resistless to destination
limbs lifted and wrung of tremor

29

Drum drum drum drum drum
then the flitting fife
peeps through

some half-imagined rhythm
drum and we cannot stay
drum and our pace quickens

outward but in another's leg
not ours a belated
fitness in an other's leg

30

A machine made of feathers
and buffed steel
plates mythed wavering in a smoke rash

cannot touch while glimpsed only
concatenation of fragments
worked into smoke out

through smoke the worst coming
glimpsed only as metonymic simmer
flakes in a rolling boil

31

Disorderly on unofficial ground
some measure of flex
scribbled cursory agendas

ad hoc for alleviation
of symptoms where they hit you gunning
from any side or pending

nice spot for a vegetable plot
clean shoots in perverse
epidemiological conditions

32

This flung in its avid face
at exactly the correct moment
in a storm of divots

exactly the right time for the project
of immobility
carried to unintelligible extremes

all thunder with a yard for swing
either side, relentless
then blown to the knackers

33

Crocked energy convulsing sideways
like a bent arrow swivelling like a weathercock
in the short run pointless

in the long run pointless too but with essential minerals
strikes a spark in the eyeball
ratified as potentiality

for a hypothetically neverending rematch
each dumbly rubbing that sore patch, tizzy
merely from having stepped in the current once

34

What hands scoped from this metal
star slammed in a thrilling dust
is almost a theology

what happens in this enclave
unfolds its elixir
in the lapse of a function

somewhere far off in a different universe altogether
coy nod in a placid cell
to our local angel of trite mischief

35

Mortal as what it clogs or limns
some gel suspended
as intimacy penetrating all

material entities, although not fully
in itself material
purely formal at the worst

here prohibitive in its thickness
suddenly now without warning
flows giving way

36

Then everything is possible
elation getting on
with the business where the business is

new qualitative adjustments
trammeled previously by a quaggy
agar in the joints

and ruts in a margin
of safety, this permissive liquor flash
flooding the anterooms

37

Simply to get as far as the nearest bush
demands the constancy of an indifferent onlooker
throat-shot or bowel-stuck so attentive you understand

in the last way or finding it part-occupied
retreat to a hidden lane
even this requiring an audacity beyond measure

all virtues depending on blood loss
in the eye as a stealing emptiness which evaluates
each move as a wonder infinite in its particularity

38

Whipped out on the dragon's thrash
each miserable segment
worm in the wyrm's breath

scorched worm in the wyrm's torched nest
each lamentable figment
scourged in a crimson sandpit

purged in a ditch
whipped back tracked charred from a burning hex
at the furnace lip

39

Hold it because given
we cannot think otherwise
or hold if we find it

simply that it has been given
or found as a given law
or that somebody wants to take it

when there is no longer anything left
to hold but a muck of slivers
will be held anyway

40

They say a king didn't want what the emperor
wants what the king didn't want the emperor
wanted the king to want

what the emperor didn't want the king
wants what the emperor didn't
want the king wanting what he

didn't know he wanted they say the king
didn't know he wanted what he didn't know
he didn't did he know what the emperor didn't know

41

When will the apples come
time's severance leaves no space
for the apples in this place

grain offers no assurance
high where it sweeps or trodden black
out of gold billed

in the fields what was promised
nixed fudged coddled fused
pulped in with the almanachs

42

I love how you love me
and this remains relevant
when almost nothing else is

I love how I love you
don't go to the baggage train
we all know what happens to the baggage train

love is no protection
you should climb a tree
be a leaf on a spirit tree

43

From rhyme to rite
from roof tree to honeysuckle bunch
the wild flames the *olden*

licking the sky's upturned basin
blackening the curve
of the vault to a reeking grot

broken gawp after the story
clamped to that whole shtum
arena of disarticulated consequences

44

Late things held in the hand last matters
considered rank physiology a momentary
flush of affections, spiritual at the edge though I think

some order flung from a great height
bells, action, belonging to nobody except me
me alone, or a rustle in corn that is mine

too and this polished stock so befitting
bouquet of comminuted photons, each last thing
mine too all of these mine

45

Eat friends eat
of this unincorporable body eat
friends eat friends

not body except
by extension
into splitter or steel goad

eat with the gut's
pricked immediacy not chewy
lippy blubber pouts and so on

46

What flourished but so must
be hard-pruned in its clarity
not later in vague aftermath

trimmed back debriding
notional surfaces materially
hacked from a doomblast

free at the point of need
still tooling away here
as light weakens surely

47

We chop them we put them out
in a dire stream
of dreck by the bucketful

they who went head
to head with a reinforced plate-glass
corner window, if not their heads

each shocked limb as a teaching aid
or many a mere lump with eyes
gob keening for reasons

48

We fix them we saw them
running at everything out in front
to trample it down flat

we fix them to teach them
frontwise, for many teeth
one bite-strap

running at everything
fixed in a fixed position
sturdy but not unassailable

49

Or if they broke there all at once
up there on the central crux
smashed hanging in rags

what came in to be
tidied up, trimmed-back
flap-sealed for the narrative

filling the carts
of a homecoming never
wholly to be grafted in

50

Before it the spike shaped to enter but in
this particularly virulent strain already cut
in a host made to measure in other worlds

already ahead of its own project, already primed
for the thrust
as raw drive hurled from a star

which ramps in a space undreamed
for each to receive as inner when its cry bores
through all codes, all remedies, only ever trivial to this point

51

As it breeds in the rafters
in the total system of fucked boiseries
bodies and soft furnishings

feeding itself out of house and home
remember the promised
oh so black comedy of return

to a niche hardly viable now
for the mission but apparently
malleable still to some domed purpose

52

Outlined against a hedge
what's smudged on the ready lips
a sore thing blotched

to the mouth's wistful corner
builds naturally in that way
slow warmth broods in the loins

the all-pervading tenderness
of a vision not yet grudged
or defiable in its mercy

53

All day squinting
clear flashes between mealy gouts
incandescent canyons

plaited through wheeling smoke-drifts
overviewed from high office
weird tumours attacked by axe-heads

this nominal decision centre
riding its gravity warp
new spouts dripping for grass

54

A feature and then a stance
umbrageously spoking
partial sightlines but let it stay

stud metal all the way up
all day considerable
watering of root and canopy

not ever fully attached
though temperamentally central
for memory with its charmed ego-system.

55

One climbs like a gouty falcon
the other's a warped tree grappling
hooks into dreamless marle

stolid intercourse with the deep
mocked by a gliding feint
from that old paladin of the skyways

later rammed in the mud beak down
as the tree leaps dancing
into a thousand miles of light

56

Beyond the square beyond the line and beyond the column
everything slides forgotten, that would be
altogether too much data to be going on with

only what is sheer and now hits the button
full-on for the forward dictum, a very symbol
nightmare clunched in a web

of futures wriggling as the threads quiver
out through unheard of reaches where a blot hangs
feeling it as a harpist the prepared glissando

57

If it would all turn out
as it must what it should
have been as seen able

where a will planed
over leagues sodden bounds
work desperate but contained

mais ça s'effiloche
misery dragging in the arse
some attention wanders

58

At first as if imagined
or imagined as something other
or wanted if not imagined

this bristling in some part nether
disequilibrium of contrived potency
knives in the blocky leaves

pages randomly flying open
what should have been unreadable
shrilling out from the crippled pulpit

59

Still to go on waiting though
while the tank empties
out of its own hollow

such subtle reverberations
barely heard but insinuated
under time's skin

the rest running out fuller
at the last a trust gathering
into a half-clenched measure

60

Striving without aim or end
that variance with itself which is essential
through solids, through voids, bolt upright in a shrivelling square

as when a claw sinks on a snout
some gormless caught in the toils
so pastoral or magnet forcing its sorcery upon iron

as man himself *homo homini lupus*
chief source of conventional and more discriminate evils
each in each each the devil in a brother

61

Not necessarily so forlorn
a body is not alone
in its seminal floret

the critical organ of a shoulder
pressed to its squirming other
in the shifting redoubt

each bosom of pale corn
light swaying brute gusts scattered
with bright summer petals

62

Held back as a shift omitted
but as if forever
held back as an open secret

forever if uncommitted
where expected, each stern eye
poised ravenous in the watch

between us this solemn ploy
held back in forever
in no time to concede that

63

Or a wish detained
from the making at any time
even apt to the circumstance

as ever if there is ever time
awaited is felt new
in the nerve's tip

at the prophesied conjunction
of selected light beams
all arrows in alignment

64

All ducks in a row
underscored by recorded precedents
a god unrolls

into grammar what cannot be
misheard or resisted
received as intended

as spoken as expended
go but the word cannot
be heard yet at this point

65

A question of innate certainty
of a march stolen
step and you carry on

a question of imposition
over fields of circumstance
a tune's gainly flow

over sprawled variable phenomena
step and a nerve bangs
down the trolley and on we go

66

A poet which is after all
exhumed trite or wholly roused by the shock
winds that bear swart musk

and then the poet already
late enough in mute
conference, inspired and disparate alchymist

lingered purrs in memorial
through the long burning
grazed on those speechless tribes

67

Before anything the banner
fixed bulb in a glory-hole
of self-abandoned shadows

banner which says no
in seductively wrought heraldry
over a tight-pegged stance

so many phantoms learning
clarity of a single pledge
so many runes an outcome

68

Like tearing or like dissolving
silently at first invisible
low pang in the unity

no drum in that ravened cleft
that breath going out then withdrawn
into the heart of terror

where no knowledge is but tearing
desire for space
where the breath is where

69

After that we were running
and that was us who
ever that was forgotten

all boneless the capped springs
squiffing out, such commotion
budding some new mad rill

lavished hard on its channel
too small far too small for the rush
ha ha we were running ha

70

I could see I was undone
a figure beyond my own
true measure but unowned

surprised in its origin
though familiar in this worn colour
coming at me grave

as if my thrown share
immaterial to that other
might fall in a different body

71

I could s   I was un one
a figure be   my own
true me   but unow ed

sur rised in its origin
though f   ar in this wo   colour
coming at me rave

as if my thro   hare
   material to that o   r
might fall in a   rent bod

72

I co ld   I was un one
a fig   be   o n
    me   but now

    rise in   in
th ug   in this   c   ur
    in   rave

    my r   are
              hat o   r
    all in a   f ren   d

73

o ld   as   one
        be   o n
   me   but

        in   in
                 this   ur
        r e

    my   ar
          t
    all   re   d

74

o   a   o e
    e   o
   e   u

     i   i
         i   u
    e

       a
      o
  a   a   e

75

The dead come apart
still singing, their attributes
resolve as rhymed sequence

draped on the mesh
or frittered as will is
messy but half on the way

to showtime, they can't help it
singing each beats
no time into gaudy shreds

76

Children we are children
none of this is happening yet
will we let it or go home

someone waits by the privet
stranger, will she let us
come home finally if we must

lips smudged at one corner
careless, would you let us would you
love would you let us anyway

77

Already the band-box witness
a protected distance
a perfumed 'kerchief

other grubbier hands rummaging
into ruination
out of ruination

objects of economic value
or pepperish sentiment
eased from a sump

78

Possibly true things coming to light later
pure archaeology of a riddle, elisions fudged
for the spiel then renewed continually as a done deal

undone here and the terroir all the jauntier for it
as the site falters under falling spicules
of evening, pollen, dust, hair, phlegm of the sickled host

compression flattening it like a water-swollen table
ever deeper into the layer, is it now our altar
our bed, this fever-mass where we lay our heats and chills

79

All that bruited high
written up in a clarion sheaf
buttering the toast

stacked in the racks
all that in a pillar
of thanksgiving

bearing no relation
framing a relation
nailing a relation

80

The sound of the ground
slowly settling the sound
of the ground

what's ground settling
in the ground settled
in the sound

slowly in the ground slowly
in the sound settling
in the settled ground

Epilogue

A Kit

81

If there must be an outcome
it will come in pieces
through several hierarchies of displacement

so many scattered engrams
if there must be an outcome
it will come in pieces

then somebody must gather them all up
and glue them, there are no
instructions on how to do that

82

Outcome implying halt
in proceedings and furthermore
a measure of containment and control

some kind of articulated lump
of grey plastic hanging
by a double-thread from the ceiling

cheers up your dearth's
daily doze, an achievement yes
but with a hollow centre

83

Neither Mustang P51
nor Alexander Calder mobile
this is your life

hung up for examination
from the prone position
quite possibly you could get inside

by means of projective fantasy
so withered and so small
the vastness of each enclosure

84

In fact an exact model of the site
which nobody who was really there
can make head or tail of

looking down as on a corpse
each dunce in their magic warp
of perceptual reverie

will of course now accept
what they're given as award
an award is an award is an award

85

Quite definitely an achievement
like one carved on a slab
or hung out like washing

telling you what was done when you dared
elusive in its intimacy
cosmic in its assent

unrelated to anything except loss
and its place in the building
half-certain while the building stands

86

Look the whole thing's 'full of stars'
so how can we resist
so clenched in our riddled inscapes

and injuries, is it true
cosmology goes on raging there
whilst here it is very quiet

folk-history of a preening thrush
each street nothing more
than a whistle to play tunes on

87

Or perhaps an exact scale model
of 'the holy ghost', threaded
on violence of an acute ray

shooting out from a cloud
through a window or some convenient
orifice in the stone work

to pierce your lolling heart
put the book down I'm giving you
this lily dipped in blood

Notes.

Page 9: 'A Ball' refers very loosely to the Duchess of Richmond's ball, which took place on 15th June, the night before the battle of Quatre Bras. Sergei Bondarchuk's film *Waterloo* (1970) makes great play with this.

Poem 2: '*rigadoon*' in this context is a form of dance-step sometimes introduced into a Quadrille, which was a dance becoming popular in Europe in the early nineteenth century.

Poem 13:
"The marigold, that goes to bed wi'th' sun,
And with him rises, weeping."
Shakespeare, *The Winter's Tale*, Act 4 Scene 4

Poem 50: There is an allusion here to the transmission mechanics of the SARS-CoV-2 virus.

Poem 54: Refers to Wellington's Tree, a natural feature near the centre of his lines, a location which he used as a kind of HQ during the battle. The tree was cut down by souvenir hunters in the aftermath.

Poem 60: warped quotes and references to Schopenhauer's *The World as Will and Idea*, via Frederick Copleston's *Arthur Schopenhauer, Philosopher of Pessimism* (Harper and Row 1975)

Poem 66: 'inspired and disparate alchymist' comes from Shelley's *Alastor*.

Poem 86: "full of stars". "Oh my God, it's full of stars" is a line from Arthur C. Clarke's novel "2001: A Space Odyssey", now also a popular internet meme. There is an interesting controversy in some circles as to whether the line actually appears in Stanley Kubrick's film of the same name, or only in the book.

Poem 87: I was thinking here of one of Carlo Crivelli's weird Annunciations.